A SKETCHBOOK DEVOTIONAL
FOR THE CREATIVE WORSHIPER

LAURA E. GOMEZ

2021

Trilogy Christian Publishers

A Wholly Owned Subsidary of Trinity Broadcasting Network

2442 Michelle Drive
Tustin, CA 92780

For information, address Trilogy Christian Publishing

Rights Department, 2442 Michelle Drive, Tustin, Ca 92780.

Trilogy Christian Publishing/ TBN and colophon are trademarks of Trinity Broadcasting Network.

For information about special discounts for bulk purchases, please contact Trilogy Christian Publishing.

Manufactured in the United States of America

Trilogy Disclaimer: The views and content expressed in this book are those of the author and may not necessarily reflect the views and doctrine of Trilogy Christian Publishing or the Trinity Broadcasting Network.

10 9 8 7 6 5 4 3 2 1

Library of Congress Cataloging-in-Publication Data is available.

ISBN 978-1-63769-036-9

ISBN 978-1-63769-037-6 (ebook)

For David, Jacob, and Matthias.

familia Gomez

TABLE OF CONTENTS

PREFACE

IN THE BEGINNING GOD CREATED

In the beginning God created the heavens and the earth" (Genesis 1:1 NIV). God is the grandmaster artist, and our life His living canvas. As Christians, we know that art does not obtain or possess any divine capabilities. God does not allow us to give power to the things created in this world. These created works of ours are not equal to God, and they do not replace God (Romans 1:25). Our art is an extension of our worship and should be used as an evangelical tool for God's glory and the furthering of His Kingdom. With that said, ultimately, my desire is that this sketchbook devotional can be used as a tool for anyone of any faith.

Whatever your creative calling may be as an artist, a poet, a songwriter, a creator—let it be for His glory alone. I pray for you, the reader, and I hope that you pray for me as well. Let us find truth together amidst the craziness and chaos that life echoes back at us. God is worthy of that.

When I became a Christian, I often found myself doodling on my devotional books and realized that my worship would pour out through my creative habits. I discovered that not only could I worship but also pray through art. I realized that, like Bezalel, God had gifted me with artistic skills for His glory and kingdom. Therefore, having visual reminders gave me encouragement and have become a great tool during trying times and spiritual battles—because art is an expression of our spirit, our soul, and our mind. Just as when the Spirit prays for us, let the Spirit speak through your art as well. Let it comfort you and renew your strength.

I encourage you to use your God-given artistic talent to further God's kingdom. You might be that church member that makes all the flyers, works on the church website, handles graphics and lyrics during services, or the one who makes the muffins to fundraise. You might be thinking you are not an artist, but this sketchbook devotional is tailored for everyone and anyone who wants to explore an additional way of worship or to have a moment of relaxation and meditation of His word.

I have Bible journaling books and whatnot, but it's a very different space when you have a guided space. I have been formatting my sketchbooks for years now and taught this method weekly at our local church under the ministry name "Praying with Paintbrushes," and people seemed to really enjoy it! Suddenly, I found myself printing out these little homemade sketchbook devotionals and giving them out during the art class.

One day, one of the ladies in the class asked me if I had ever thought of turning this into a book? Funny enough, I never had. I went home and prayed about it, and then life's storms hit. My mother-in-law battled cancer for almost two years, and my husband had battles of his own, but God sustained us through it all. Then we went through life's milestones of our oldest son moving out to go to college and finding out that a thirteen-year-old prayer was finally answered. We were pregnant. At forty, it was a high-risk pregnancy with tons of challenges, but our baby boy was finally born safe and healthy. It had now been roughly five years since that prayer, and God brought me back here, to this book. It is your book now to doodle in, to save your poetic moments, thoughts, your processes, and to create as you may during your journey.

I write to you whole heartedly, and my hope for you, the reader, is that you use this sketchbook to worship and express your faith, healing, hopes, prayers, and all of your creativity through art for His glory alone. To use this book for those moments when words are hard to find or just when you are feeling that creative itch. The instructions on some of these creative prompts are for drawing and sketching, *but* if you would rather express yourself by writing, etc., that is awesome too. All we do requires some form of creativity... so go on—create!

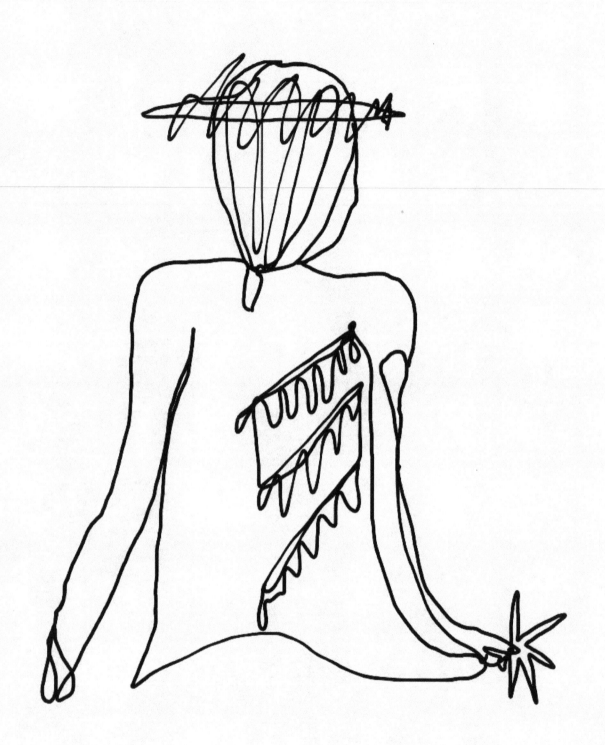

STRIPES + HEALING

I'm hurt and in pain; Give me space for healing, and mountain air.

(Psalm 69:29 MSG)

We will begin with a more intimate exercise of our sketchbook. This part of the devotional is completely voluntary. I have had a person or two not participate because they simply were not yet ready. If this is you, I respect your season and your journey, and you can skip along and come back later or not. There is this belief that we have to be perfectly healed before God can use us, and that is simply not true. Sometimes the damaged parts of us are what God uses because He is at His strongest when we are at our weakest. Broken crayons still draw straight lines, but this is your space. Here we go...

At a young age, I had a very traumatic experience—I was assaulted. It took many, many years of rebellious, reckless, ungodly behavior until one day, God "knocked me off my horse" per se and brought me to my knees. You see, I use to believe that there was no God and that if there was, all these terrible things would not be happening. I didn't have an understanding of this fallen world, of good vs. evil. However, when God removed the veil and allowed me to see with spiritual eyes, not only was I a believer, but I could now allow God to begin to heal my heart, mind, and spirit. I went through professional spiritual and secular counseling—healing center prayer meetings. A slew of tears and oceans of regrets, but eventually, I received closure, and much of me was healed by the stripes of our glorious Savior!

We are all in different seasons of our life, so if you are going through a season of healing, I want to share an exercise that has helped me wait and cope with hope. I have done this exercise about a dozen times—a zillion times. All with different sketches, situations, and outcomes, but it was SO incredibly therapeutic. You might think you need a whole reem of paper, and if that is the case, then by all means.

The next two pages are blank. On one page, write down or draw those emotional things that still spark pain. Once you are done, you can do one of three things. You can cover everything in red paint, markers, or your favorite media. The red artistically represents the blood of Christ absorbing your pain. Second, you can tear out the page and shred it or dispose of it as you wish. This has been my favorite thing. There is something very satisfying about tearing paper containing my pain, emotions, and traumas. Third, keep it in your private sketchbook and continue to pray over it. Sometimes healing happens in a moment; other times, it is a long season, and other times, it is our thorn to bear. Christ bared it all on the cross so that we would not have to carry all this pain around. Give it to Him. I pray that this exercise gets you a little closer to experiencing His healing. He loves so much that He died for you, for me, for us—for an attainable eternity. Parts of me are still healing, and that is perfectly ok because one day, He will completely heal us all! He will make us perfect in His eternal glory!

16

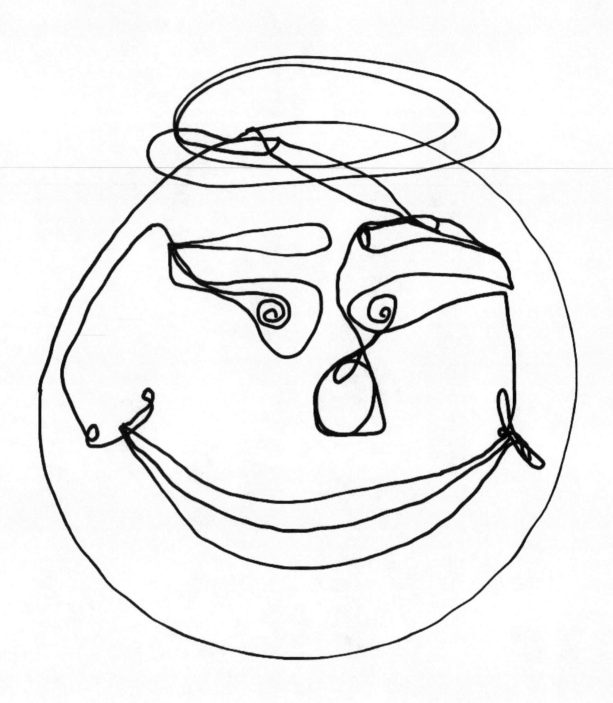

JOY + STRENGTH

I've told you these things for a purpose: that my joy might be your joy, and your joy wholly mature.

(John 15:11–15 MSG)

Joy is a **powerful choice!** For as long as I can remember, art has always brought me so much joy! No matter what was happening around me, I knew that I could grab my paintbrushes and pencils to express what I could not speak out loud. Joy is a choice that we make regardless of our circumstances. Happiness consists of our circumstances. When we choose joy, we are choosing strength. I would draw and paint things or moments that brought me joy. My little drawings would take me back to the scripture that inspired that piece of artwork, and once I was back to the word of God, I would feel refocused on Him and His purpose for my life. As is said in *Nehemiah 8:10, "...Do not grieve, for the joy of the Lord is your strength" (NIV).*

So, this next page is blank for you, the reader, to create something that brings you joy! You will be surprised by the things that will come to mind. I once taught this class at church, and one student drew a cup of coffee because it reminded them of morning devotionals and their time with the Lord. I myself once drew a bowl of white rice because it reminded me of when I was around five or six-years-old cooking with my godmother. She taught me how to make steamed rice for Sunday dinner, and I was ecstatic to be cooking with her and with the idea of feeling so grown up.

Let us take a moment to close our eyes, take a deep breath, and meditate on God's word. What images come to mind when you think about the word "JOY"? Let the Lord fill you with joy and allow His word to refocus you on His purpose for your life.

20

22

POETRY + GOD

Sometimes

Sometimes the sun doesn't shine
so bright anymore, and the stars seem dim
and the moon doesn't glow over the dull gray nighttime clouds.
Sometimes, just sometimes, the heartaches a little more than usual
and tears pour out a bit more than usual,
and sometimes we just have to say goodbye
to people that mattered and to things that don't matter anymore,
and sometimes our smiles may not stretch out as far as they use to,
but You, Lord, You forever shine brighter than the brightest star
and brighter than the brightest day
lighting up my heart and drying my eyes.
Sometimes, just sometimes, it is good to remind ourselves that in the morning
the sun will shine brighter, and the stars will be invisible
but still somewhere in the sky.

My Heart

Prepare my heart, my Lord, to laugh when there is joy
And to cry when there is pain and peace when there is none.
Prepare my heart, my Lord, to sing where there is praise
And lift my hands in time of prayer and strength when weak.
Prepare my heart, my Lord, when my spirit breaks
To be with You when I am alone and have love when I felt none.
Prepare my heart, my Lord, to walk through deep valleys
To be still throughout the storm and have faith in the unseen.
Prepare my heart, my Lord, to give where there is need
To feel when others hurt and rejoice when others celebrate.
Prepare my heart, my Lord, to sail Your rough seas
To walk the golden streets and in the end to see Your face.

SPANISH POEM
(ENGLISH TRANSLATION ON NEXT PAGE):

Flor en el Desierto

Yo era como una flor en el desierto que una vez dormía

Que no tenía propósito y no tenía alegría

Me desvestía de mis pétalos para encontrar la aprobación

De hombres que pagaban con golpes y destrucción

Yo nomas quería una gota de agua viva pero Fe yo no tenía y a Dios yo no le creía

Un día esa flor estuvo al punto de completamente desaparecer casi enterada en la tierra

Pero Jesus mando la lluvia y esa flor volvió a renacer

Una nueva gracia brillaba la santidad me llamaba

La palabra me hablaba ahora mi corazón con gozo lloraba

La flor que antes no valía nada yo no sabía que con tus vientos me caresiavas

No sabía que con el sol mi vida tú cuidabas y con las estrellas

de los cielos cada noche me arrullabas a esta flor más fea esta flor más susia

Esta flor más seca que Jesús también murió por ella

Y por la cruz esta flor fue: Justificada, Santificada, Bautizada y Regenerada

Ahora camino bajo la sombra del altísimo camino en ese lugar santísimo

Ahora camino al lado de la rosa de sharon de el lirio de las valles que me canta una canción

Florecerás hija mía, florecerás! Te e plantado en la orilla de los ríos y del mar

Con Jesús a mi lado esta flor en el desierto nunca más se secará

Florecerás hija mía, florecerás! florecerás!

A Desert Flower

I was like a flower in the desert that once slept and that had no purpose and had no joy.

I was stripped of petals to find approval from men who paid with hurt and destruction.

I just wanted a drop of living water, but I did not have faith or belief in God.

This flower was at the point of dying and buried deep in the earth.

But Jesus sent the rain and that flower was reborn and a new grace was shining over her .

And holiness was calling her, the word spoke into my heart and with joy cried.

This flower that was worth nothing did not know that with your winds you would caress her.

And that you cared for her life with the sun and she did not know that every night you lulled her With the stars from the heavens, this ugliest flower, this dirty flower,

This flower that had dried out in the sun, Jesus also died for her and by the cross

this flower was: Justified, Sanctified, Baptized, Regenerated

Now I walk under the shadow of the highest into that most holy place.

Now I walk beside the Rose of Sharon, with the lily of the valley that sings me a song.

"You will blossom my daughter, you will blossom!

I have planted you on the shore of the rivers and of the sea!"

With Jesus by my side, this flower in the desert will never dry up again

"You will blossom my daughter! You will flourish! You will flourish!"

On this next page, you get to be the poet! Do not worry; as you can see, I am not much of a poet myself, but writing like this really helps me express my inner thoughts and struggles to our beloved God. My prayer is that below you allow yourself to do the same.

GOD + YOUR HEART

Prepare my heart, my Lord, to

and to_____when_____

Prepare my heart, my Lord, to_____

And lift my hands_____

Prepare my heart, my Lord, when_____

To be with You when_____

Prepare my heart, my Lord, to_____

To be still through_____and_____

Prepare my heart, my Lord, when_____

To_____when_____

Prepare my heart, my Lord, to_____

To walk the golden streets and in the end to see Your face.

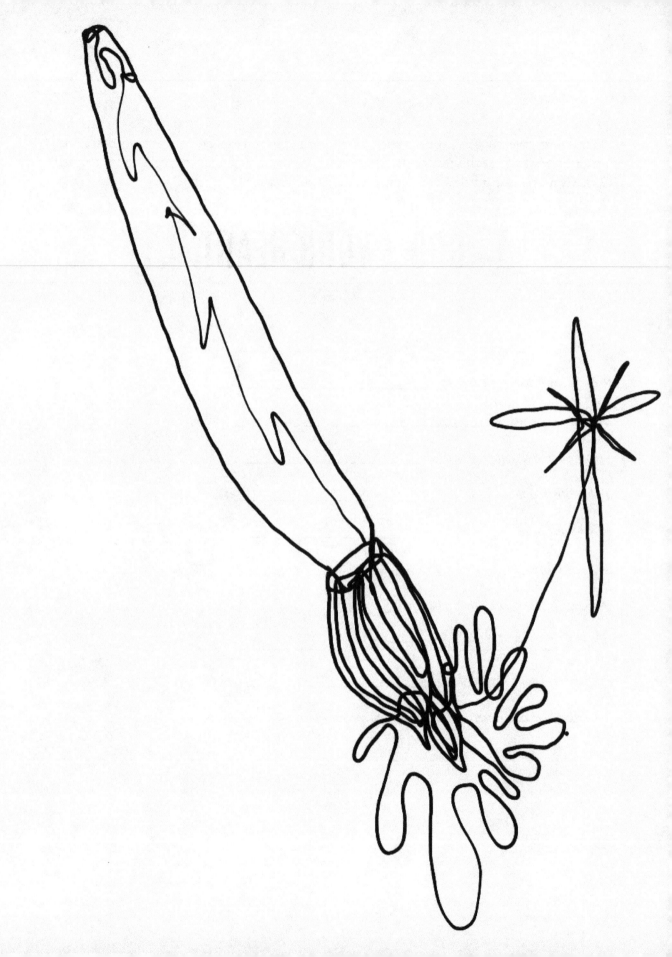

CREATIVITY + PRAYER

If we don't know how or what to pray, it doesn't matter. He does our praying in and for us, making prayer out of our wordless sighs, our aching groans. He knows us far better than we know ourselves, knows our pregnant condition, and keeps us present before God. That's why we can be so sure that every detail in our lives of love for God is worked into something good.

(Romans 8:26–28 MSG)

I am a visual learner and using my creativity alongside prayer has kept me present before God. The Holy Spirit makes prayer out of our "wordless" moments. It also keeps me constantly searching the Scriptures so that I may continue to learn and know God more. It helps me relax and actually focus on what I am praying about.

There is quite a difference between praying about something and sitting there with my art supplies and sitting there with my prayers right in front of me. Prayer requires a great deal of imagination. It is not difficult to pray because we have been given guidelines. Jesus gave us a beautiful template in Matthew 6:9, which begins with "Father". It was not how the Pharisees prayed, but Jesus got creative because He was here to show us how it was done, and He wants us to use our imagination when we pray and not just repeat the same prayer over and over. In doing this, your creativity can develop and spill into other areas of your life. These next few pages are blank for you and your prayers—to sketch them out, to jot down keywords, or express them through poetry or doodles. It is your space now.

30

32

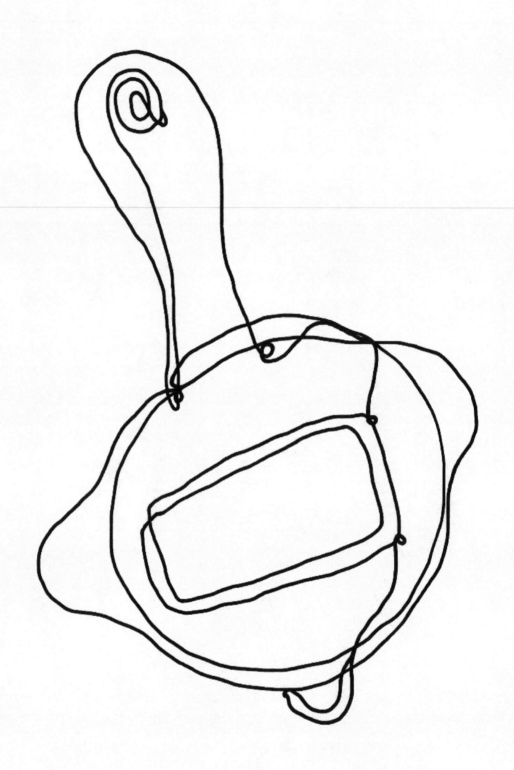

BRICK + SKILLET

Now, son of man, take a brick and place it before you. Draw a picture of the city Jerusalem on it. Then make a model of a military siege against the brick: Build siege walls, construct a ramp, set up army camps, lay in battering rams around it. Then get an iron skillet and place it upright between you and the city—an iron wall. Face the model: The city shall be under siege and you shall be the besieger. This is a sign to the family of Israel.

(Ezekiel 4:1–3 MSG)

Symbolism is often used throughout the Bible. It helps give meaning and sparks emotion. Here we see Ezekiel using a clay brick or "tablet" to represent Jerusalem. It is believed that the name "Jerusalem" was inscribed on the clay. These bricks were used to build Babylon's walls and buildings. God is instructing and warning Ezekiel of the impending judgment and discipline. The iron skillet most likely represented the people's resistance to Ezekiel's message.

On this next page, you will draw a clay brick and a skillet. You can add all the other details from the scripture if you want to be extra creative but at least draw the two items. To me, these two have been a great reminder of the importance of obedience to the word of God and to the men and women that God has placed over me as His representatives. They are powerful reminders to allow ourselves to be open to growth, change, advice, and that there are consequences when we think we know best. It is incredibly humbling. Take a deep breath, pray, and let the Spirit guide your hands—now draw.

36

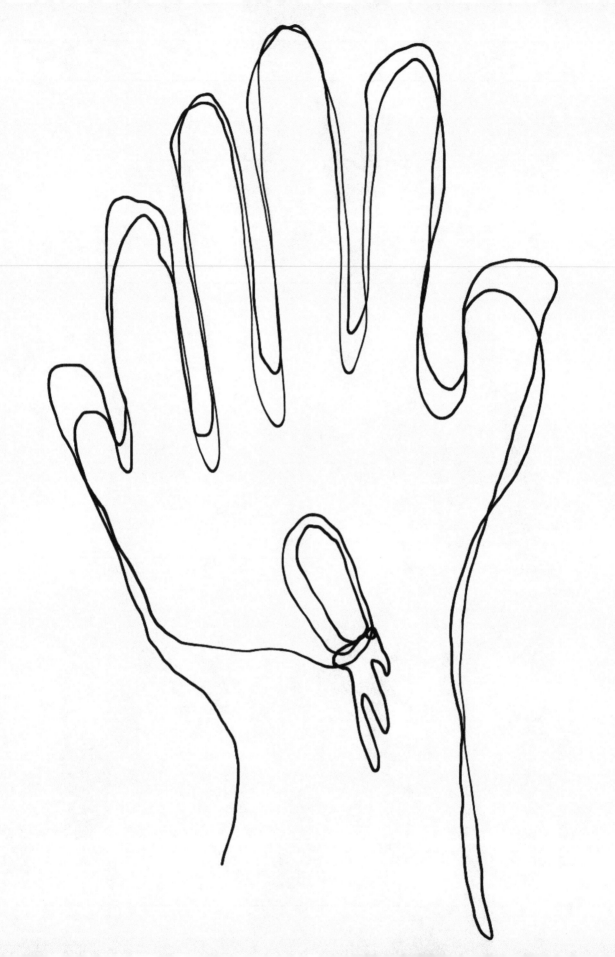

CRUCIFIED + LIVING

Christ lives in me. The life you see me living is not "mine," but it is lived by faith in the Son of God, who loved me and gave himself for me. I am not going to go back on that. Is it not clear to you that to go back to that old rule-keeping, peer-pleasing religion would be an abandonment of everything personal and free in my relationship with God? I refuse to do that, to repudiate God's grace. If a living relationship with God could come by rule-keeping, then Christ died unnecessarily.

(Galatians 2:20–21MSG)

No longer do we live, but Christ lives in us and through us. The life we live is not to please others but to serve others. Everyone is called to follow the one that is perfect even when we are not. We are humans living in a fallen world, so fall we will, but we get up because it is not about us anymore. We are crucified with Him and are His vessel here on this earth to align our will with His will. For this next activity, you will need pencils. You can use a regular pencil, sketching pencils, and even charcoal if that's your thing.

1. On the next sketchbook page, trace your hand to cover most of the page.

2. Take a long look at the inside of your hand, palm, and fingers.

3. Draw all those little details of the inside of your hand—every line, wrinkle, scar, mole—all of it.

4. Behind your hand, you will draw a beam of wood. Think of the angle of a hand extended over the tip of a cross.

5. Draw an opening or a nail in the middle of your drawn hand. Add blood flowing from the pierced areas.

6. The end result is your hand crucified with Christ. It is as if you drew the hand of our Lord crucified but with your hand.

I know it is a bit unsettling to see a part of ourselves crucified with Christ on paper in a simple sketch. That is the power of art. It is no longer just a scripture; it is a created image that will forever remind us of His sacrifice specifically for you, me, and everyone. Our relationship with Him is so personal, yet we can all have access to Him if we just accept Him. The omnipresent power of our creator is enthralling! He is in everything and in the everywhere of space and time. My prayer for you is that you use this next page to connect with your creator, and this exercise will allow you to get closer to aligning your will with His will. Step into His space and be crucified with Him. Allow Him to continue to live through you. His will is perfect, and He loves us unconditionally even when we are far, far from perfection.

ART + AFFIRMATIONS

A wise person gets known for insight; gracious words add to one's reputation.
(Proverbs 16:21 MSG)

Gracious speech is like clover honey—good taste to the soul, quick energy for the body.
(Proverbs 16:24 MSG)

For as he thinks in his heart, so is he.

(Proverbs 23:7 NKJV)

I must be honest; I was not a big fan of affirmations. I thought they were silly and useless, but it was not until my husband began to exercise them that I noticed that maybe there was something to them. Proverbs 16:21 talks about insight, a deep understanding of something. In verse 24, it talks about gracious words being good and energy to the soul, and Proverbs 23:7 speaks about not who we are but who we think of ourselves to be. If I live my life according to how I see myself, I am in dire trouble because I am humanly flawed and damaged… BUT if I live my life according to how God sees me, life can be a blessed event. Affirmations do just that! There is power in positive words about us. If we are constantly putting ourselves down and thinking that we "cannot," then we will not. If we are constantly reminding ourselves that we are:

1. I am the APPLE of God's eye *(Psalm 17)*.

2. I am the reason for the CROSS *(John 3:16)*.

3. I am a CHILD of a King *(Galatians 4:5)*.

4. I am part of a CHOSEN generation *(1 Peter 2:9)*.

5. I am His ANOINTED *(Acts 10:38)*.

6. I am ETERNALLY rewarded *(Psalm 37:18)*.

7. I am made to be GREAT *(Psalm 91:14)*!

8. I am LOVED *(Jeremiah 31:3)*.

9. I am BRAVE *(Hebrews 13:6)*.

10. I am FEARLESS *(Isaiah 41:13)*.

11. I am VALUABLE *(Luke 12:24 + Luke 12:7)*.

12. I lack NOTHING *(Philippians 4:19)*.

13. I am PROSPEROUS *(Psalm 1:3 + 2 Chronicles 26:5)*.

14. My JOY cannot be robbed! *(John 16:22)*!

15. I am in HIS PRESENCE *(Psalm 16:11)*.

16. I have PEACE *(Isaiah 55:12)*.

This next page is for you to make a collage of your affirmations by clipping photos, magazine images, add doodles, glue, paint, and fabric—it's all good when it comes to collaging. Pray and be still and hear God's soft loving voice. His thoughts and words of you are good and positive. Draw close to Him, and He will draw close to you (pun intended). Make it great and make it fun!

ART + THE GOSPEL

How can we picture God's kingdom? What kind of story can we use?

(Mark 4:30 MSG)

Once upon a time, I attended an impressive museum exhibit that had on display these beautiful large church window panels. Each panel had a chronological painting of the story of Jesus Christ. The panels told His complete story of His birth, life, death, and resurrection. The panels had aged beautifully with chipping and fading paint on parts of the weathered wood. They stood under a low light, which is common with very old artwork. They declared a very powerful story that created a golden silence in the room and atmosphere.

I couldn't take my eyes off other people's facial expressions and reactions. The subtle lifting of their brows and the positioning of their hand under their chin as they pondered the images. I couldn't help but wonder what these panels were doing to their spirit and their soul. I was experiencing that old saying about pictures and the thousand words. I soon learned that in the olden times, the less fortunate did not know how to read. Therefore, churches would have these paintings to tell the story of the Gospel to those that could not read. What an amazing way for art to be used for God's glory.

On these next few pages, take a moment to think about the Gospel and tell the great story with your art! The life, death, and resurrection of our Lord Christ Jesus. These pages are yours, the reader, the artist, the creative worshiper.

48

50

52

BLOOM + BLOOM SOME MORE

...When your patience is finally in full bloom, then you will be ready for anything, strong in character, full and complete.

(James 1:4 TLB)

Like many, I too love flowers, and I love plants! but for me, both are hard to grow and maintain. They require a lot of waiting and nurturing, but they, in turn, do teach a lot of patience!

There are so many biblical parallels in the Bible to planting and reaping. There is the well-known parable of the seed, and it falls amongst the different types of soil. This scripture is referencing our patience in "full bloom," which also happens to be one of the fruits of the Spirit and describes in part—love. Patience is one of the most important virtues and character traits to have as a Christian. It not only tests our faith, but it stretches it out. The Bible tells us how David waited and prayed to the Lord with his "life a prayer". WOW! Now that is waiting with all of your heart and all of your soul and all of your mind! In this psalm, David declares,

> *I pray to GOD—my life a prayer—and wait for what he'll say and do. My life is on the line before God, my Lord, waiting and watching till morning, waiting and watching till morning.*
>
> *(Psalm 130:5–6 MSG)*

You will know that God is bringing your patience to full bloom when you notice that you no longer react the same way you did before. I recently learned that a part of a seed actually dies before it begins to grow. I like to think that the part of our seed that dies is all the things that do not help us grow—Things such as doubt, fear, hate, and pretty much all of those things listed in Galatians that speak of the lusts of the flesh. If you wait on Him and constantly seek the presence of the Holy Spirit and His guidance, you will be filled with patience and all of those other fruits. Like the Bible also says in Galatians, love is patient and fruitful proof of walking in the spiritual.

So, not only will you bloom, but you will produce spiritual fruit and become walking proof of our living God. Whether that fruit is by bringing others to the Lord, getting more involved at your local church or ministry, your fruit will produce more fruit, and so on. The best time to bloom is often when troubles and obstacles arise... those are the moments when we have to choose to wait for the Lord. His time is not our time. For me, it was time when I have felt the most alone, but I was not really alone—we are never truly alone with God in control of our life. The Lord was always with me and He is always with you. Sometimes God needs to separate us from the things around us so that our focus and patience are centered around Him! When a seed grows, it does so in the deep, dark soil, and when it's ready, part of it dies, it rises to the surface and looks around and sees that all the other flowers are blooming right along with it. That is how it is in this Christian walk. You are never alone; you are just growing quietly in the dark.

In this next exercise, I want you to close your eyes, take a deep breath and write out, or, as always, you can draw out the areas of your life that you think you could use some more patience. For me, I have had to learn to pause and think before I react. I can be impulsive at times with how I react to situations, and I have not yet mastered it, but I am working on it always. Art and writing help me do just that. It slows me down and helps me reflect. Our entire life is a constant prayer that awaits our beautiful, loving, and wonderful Lord. Breathe, be still, and wait for Him to tell you what to say and what to do. He is right there with you.

love

joy

peace

patience

kindness

goodness

faithfulness

gentleness

self-control

THE FRUIT + THE SPIRIT

But the fruit of the Spirit is love, joy, peace, longsuffering, kindness, goodness, faithfulness, gentleness, self-control. Against such there is no law.

(Galatians 5:22–23 NKJV)

A fruitful list that for a long time made a lovely piece of artwork and desk décor. You would think that the positive interactions with others are what sparked a certain observation, but unfortunately, this is not the case. I witnessed an interaction between two ladies at church one day that stopped me in my tracks.

We were having a bake sale and one of the young ladies from church brought the same type of cake as another one of the older ladies. She walked into the church foyer with a youthful, peppy spirit. She was proud of her cake as she should have been because it was delicious! Her cake sold out in minutes while the older sister's cake was slowly selling. The young woman was so kind that she went over to the table and purchased a slice herself in hopes to lift her sister's spirit. Unfortunately, her kindness was unfairly dismissed. The older sister made a remark, and I just saw the young woman's smile completely drop off her face. I have no idea what was said, but the expressions on their faces spoke a million words, and the first thing that popped into my mind was, "one of those sisters is not walking in the spirit." I know it's a harsh judgment to pass, but it was not the first time I observed this older sister being unkind. I later learned from her that she was going through some hard times, and her emotions got the best of her. She had not been attending prayer meetings, services, and was also skipping fellowship events. All of those things help us stay on that spiritual path where we walk with the Spirit and not in the flesh.

This next page is for you to express either areas that you feel need spiritual improvement or what the fruit of the Spirit looks like to you. It is hard to always stay in the Spirit, but God has given it to us as a gift to HELP us along the way and help us navigate through this imperfect world. I pray that if any of the fruits are lacking in your life as they can in mine, I pray that not only can you find them, but in them, you will flourish.

60

62

LONELINESS + FEELINGS

Don't panic. I'm with you. There's no need to fear for I'm your God. I'll give you strength. I'll help you. I'll hold you steady, keep a firm grip on you.

(Isaiah 41:10 MSG)

Loneliness is not new to any of us, and though the reasons for loneliness vary from person to person, we have all fallen into its familiar trap. Please know that it is only temporary and with purpose. Some of us have suffered traumas, some have been hurt by someone they trusted, and others just feel alone because of other circumstances. Whatever the situation, we must not panic and confront loneliness bearing the full amour. Once we understand that loneliness is just another fiery arrow from the enemy, we can have a better handle on the entire situation.

God most undeniably understands your loneliness. He has felt it, He has breathed it, and it has hurt Him as much as it hurt us. He ultimately died alone on a cross, abandoned and wounded. He knows loneliness better than anyone. God has given us the tools to combat our feelings because they are unreliable. Instead of isolating ourselves even further to be devoured by the roaming lion, we need to reach out and be transparent. Ask for prayer from at least one trusted person.

By now, you're probably wondering where the "art part" of this is—we're almost there. I started planting my own little herb garden from the very beginning with seeds and soil and all. During this newfound hobby (that I am terrible at, by the way ...shh), I realized how impatient I could get. I would plant the little seed in the soil, waited days, and nothing. A few more days, nothing. I wanted to dig a little into the dirt and see what was going on, but I did not want to kill the little seed, so I waited. After almost two weeks, I started seeing the little sprouts pop up, and I was so excited!

It is kind of like that with God. Sometimes He needs to place us in a little soil by ourselves so that we grow. This Christian business is all about growing, being formed, being shaped, molded, you name it. It is the constant beat of the Christian life—change. He will continue to transform us and sometimes break us down and build us up again because He loves us. One day we will all be made perfect and share eternity with Him. For now, we just have to keep living and keep growing.

I hope my tiny little insights offered up some encouragement. In this next activity, we are going to break out some colored pencils. I want you to sketch a seed growing inside some soil—any seed you want. Roots sprouting, no roots; however your mind is visualizing it. You are that seed. God is working on you. You are not alone. He is here. I am here with you somehow through this sketchbook. I have faith that with God's help, you, too, will overcome moments of loneliness. I did, and so have many others. God is always shining down on you, and at His time, you too will bloom. I am rooting for you! (Pun intended)

SEASONS + FRIENDSHIP

Friends love through all kinds of weather, and families stick together in all kinds of trouble.

(Proverbs 17:7 MSG)

Right now, for me, it is the year 2020, and there is a worldwide pandemic. The political climate is definitely something, and it has brought out the worst in some people—some even our friends. I am not a political mind. I have long accepted the fact that this world is not my home, but I do what I can; biblically. I have also come to accept that we do not all think alike, and not only do our politics differ from person to person but so do our theologies.

So, what do we do? For me, it has worked to agree to disagree and love my friends, regardless. If they choose to unfriend me, I will respect that choice, but if we are going to continue to be friends, then we need to have grace for one another. We MUST love our friends through all kinds of weather because that is how God loves us. I recently lost one of my best friends to COVID-19, so I say this with all sincerity; you never know when a friend will be taken away. Always have grace for all of your friends, especially the ones you may not see eye to eye with. Grace has been given freely to us, and we are entrusted by our God to be generous with that grace towards others. A friend loves at all times. I do not know if, by now, things are better or not by the time you, the reader, are engaging in this sketchbook, but I pray that they are because right now, life is short.

This next activity involves praying for and drawing one of your friends and maybe a "not so friend," and take a look at the season that you see that your friend is going through or that they overcame. Then, take a picture of your work and send it to that friend and let them know you are praying for them. Life is tough, and I have always felt that little extra encouragement when I have received a little note or gift from a friend and even more from a person I didn't think liked me all that much. Sometimes I have received them from someone I least expected it from. Maybe God wants you to do it for a person that was once a friend, but He has placed that person in your heart. As with music, art is also about reaching up, reaching in, and reaching out. This glorifies God, and it lets us know that not only is God with us, but that He is not just our Lord our Savior, but also our friend.

Write out a prayer for your special friend:

68

PETER + THE BOAT

He said, "Come ahead." Jumping out of the boat, Peter walked on the water to Jesus.

(Matthew 14:29 MSG)

We all have talents that have been gifted by God. Some of those talents we are well aware of, and others may still be hidden deep inside. Perhaps due to fear of failure, lack of confidence, or just remains yet to be uncovered. We will not know until we get out of the boat, spiritually speaking, of course. This scripture has been an inspiration for me personally. I have tried and failed at many of my endeavors, but I kept pressing on. I have stepped out of my boat time and time again and felt like I was walking with Jesus on the water before I sank. When we think we are drowning, He lifts us up and out of the water—always.

Some people may view Peter sinking was out of lacking faith, but to me, it's a great accomplishment to trust when Jesus says "come," and we go. And yet, other people never get out of the boat and try something new with Christ. Others believe that if you do not succeed, it was not His will in the first place. I also disagree with that point of view because all things work for good to those who love the Lord (Romans 8:28). It is often in these times of "failure" that God teaches us some valuable lessons. Failure can be a strength because that is when we are at our weakest and He at His strongest. So please never feel that failure lessens your being because it does not. We dust off the dirt, we strap on our boots, and we press on.

In this next activity, draw a boat floating over a sea of your dreams, hopes, endeavors, and draw yourself walking over them; draw those real, raw thoughts and pray over them. Pray that God leads you to develop, discover, or flourish in the talents and gifts that He has given to you. Ask and you will get. God is so loving and giving that you should embrace your failures and pat yourself on the back for being brave enough to step out of the boat and into the unknown. God will lead your way, and if you sink, He will rescue you, He will pull you out and take you up to safety.

72

STUMBLING BLOCKS +
THE VICTORY

Then Jesus went to work on his disciples. "Anyone who intends to come with me has to let me lead. You're not in the driver's seat; I am. Don't run from suffering; embrace it. Follow me and I'll show you how. Self-help is no help at all. Self-sacrifice is the way, my way, to finding yourself, your true self. What kind of deal is it to get everything you want but lose yourself? What could you ever trade your soul for?

Matthew 16:24–26 (MSG)

Like many doubters before me, I, too, was once an atheist with pretty extensive Bible knowledge, but I refused to believe. Rather, I did not want to believe that there was a God out there that one day would judge how I lived my life according to my own beliefs. I had become my own stumbling block. When I became a Christian, I wanted desperately to blame the culture, the age of reason and pretty much anything and anyone outside of myself. It was not anyone or anything's fault other than myself and my own terrible choices.

I had grown up in church, I knew the Gospel, but I made a choice not to believe. I was around twelve years old and I made the choice to leave the church and abandoned my faith all by myself. I got tired of the church version of "mean girls," and I fell into Satan's trap! The old "those church girls are mean and lack God's love, and therefore there is no God" mentality. I saw those girls as my stumbling blocks, but really it was my own lack of understanding. As a woman of faith, now it all sounds quite silly, but back then, it was a serious belief ruled by my emotions. Was my walking away truly their fault? Most definitely not; it was mine. Life is ten percent what happens to us and ninety percent how we respond. I declined to respond according to biblical principles. I took everything so personally and lost sight of who God was. It is something I struggle with even now. The only difference today is that I refuse to walk away from my faith based on the actions of other imperfect humans because I myself am flawed. When we read the interactions between God and humanity, we will find a plethora of imperfections and failures. The only perfect one is Christ Jesus, our Lord. What is your true stumbling block? What can your self-sacrifice be to overcome it? Draw it out and let God give you the victory over it!

76

CHURCH + DOORS

The two doors also were of olive tree; and he carved upon them carvings of cherubims and palm trees and open flowers, and overlaid them with gold, and spread gold upon the cherubims, and upon the palm trees.

(1 Kings 6:32 KJV)

I would never have guessed how important church doors would be to me in this present time. It is true that we take the tiny little things for granted. Right now, as I write this book, churches across the country, and quite possibly the world, are closed. Right now, in my time, there is a worldwide pandemic, and depending on what point in time you have acquired this book, church doors may be open or still closed. As my husband and I drove by our little Westmorland, CA church, the doors had caught my eye. The church sits almost at the corner of the street and is well visible if you were stopped by the red traffic light. It was during the first shut-down in March of 2020. It was surreal and unexpected. We have to drive by it on the way to the store. While we sat there waiting for the light to turn green, I kept getting flashbacks of opening those doors to enter for Sunday service, choir practice, a women's Bible study, and other numerous activities. I actually cried as I remembered thinking that all this would be over soon, that we would all be going back to normal, and we would be walking through those doors once again—it is now January 2021 for me and thinking about it is incredibly still heartbreaking.

I have NEVER missed church doors so much in my life, and I would NEVER have thought that would be a thing to feel. I never thought doors would purge hot tears from my eyes and make them roll down my face. At this point, I had to search for a picture of them because I could not remember what my church doors looked like. I was reading my Bible and came across 1 Kings 6:32 and the beautiful detail Solomon had for the doors of the temple. Our church doors are not so fancy, but they do not have to be because their value is still quite immeasurable. Sketch your church doors. I know drawing them cannot and will not replace being there, but I pray that sketching them can be a little breath of sweet air for your soul.

80

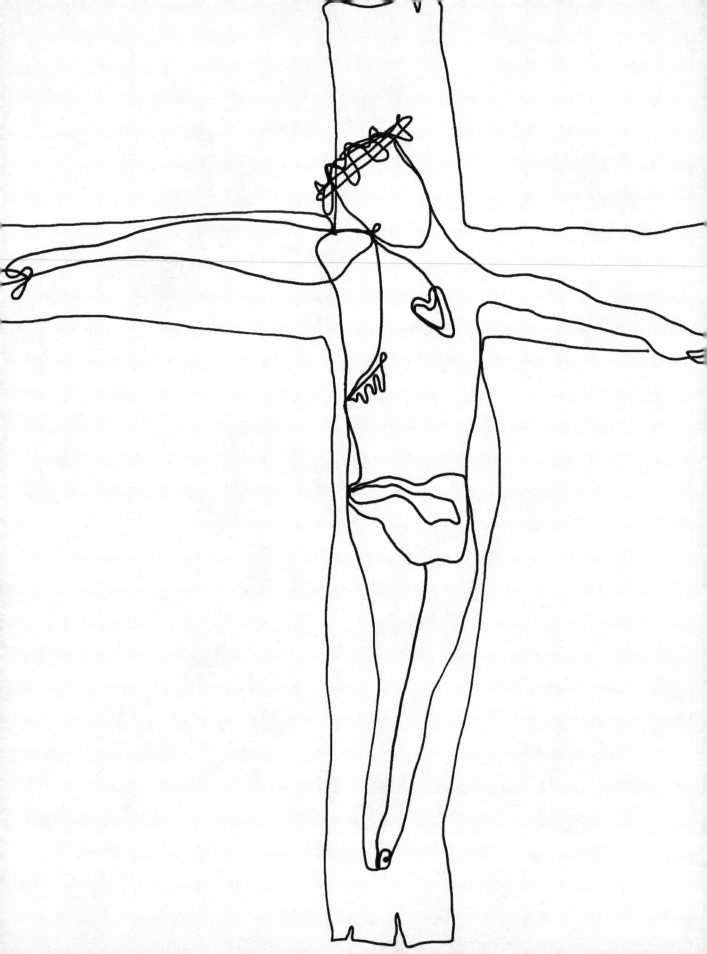

GOD + COLLAGING

Because of this decision we don't evaluate people by what they have or how they look. We looked at the Messiah that way once and got it all wrong, as you know. We certainly don't look at him that way anymore. Now we look inside, and what we see is that anyone united with the Messiah gets a fresh start, is created new. The old life is gone; a new life burgeons! Look at it! All this comes from the God who settled the relationship between us and him, and then called us to settle our relationships with each other. God put the world square with himself through the Messiah, giving the world a fresh start by offering forgiveness of sins. God has given us the task of telling everyone what he is doing. We're Christ's representatives. God uses us to persuade men and women to drop their differences and enter into God's work of making things right between them. We're speaking for Christ himself now: Become friends with God; he's already a friend with you.

(2 Corinthians 5:17–20 MSG)

We are new creatures in Christ, without a doubt! We are born again in God's grace, and that means the old way of seeing ourselves has to die too. People from our past and sometimes the people from our present will want to treat us as our old selves, and though we ought to never forget what God has brought us out of, it does not mean to keep making decisions as our old selves. I know it is hard for some like me that have had quite the past, but it is not impossible with God and His word.

I did this visual board activity at church once, and on it, we had to do a collage (take clippings of photos, magazines, etc., to use as art media) of what we wanted our lives to look like. Of course, I clipped images of a nice home, car, and job. The instructor told me I did a nice job, but I had overlooked what I wanted to be on this vision board. I ended up making a collage of the old me and the new me. The old collage had clippings of my past life; drugs, alcohol, and pretty much a life of debauchery. My new life had clippings of churches, clouds, mountains, love, hope, crosses, and anything that could relate visually to a Christ-centered life. Even though I lived a life of sin, God always saw me how I visualized myself on that other side of the collage. I did not only see the old me in that collage, but I saw the fresh start that was possible because of what Christ did on that cross. The contrast was quite shocking, and I honestly felt embarrassed of my past. I do not know where that collage is now, but that day it got passed around to everyone, and God was glorified; that's what really matters.

When we see ourselves as God sees us, we are accepting and allowing ourselves to continue God's transformation. We can understand and embrace our imperfections and our brokenness because Christ died for them too—to give us a new life and to be who God saw in us all along. I encourage you to use the next couple of pages to collage your old self and then your new self; then let God be glorified!

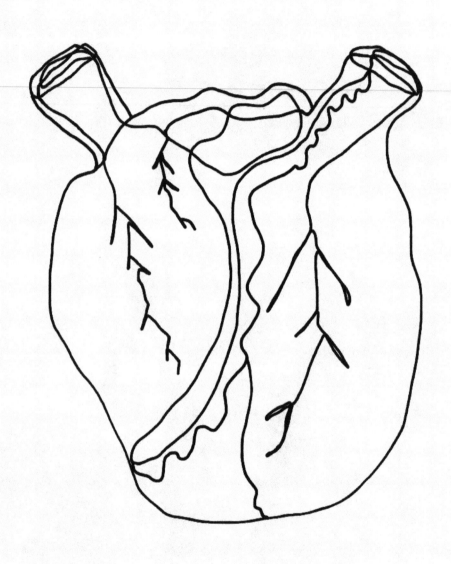

INTENTIONS + A PURE HEART

The goal of this command is love, which comes from a pure heart and a good conscience and a sincere faith.

(1 Timothy 1:5 NIV)

I do not know for sure, but I imagine this is the scripture that inspired the phrase "check your heart!" This phrase has sparked laughter and controversy all at the same time. Paul is writing to Timothy all sorts of information on the logistics of ministry, worship, and sound doctrine. I am in no way a theologian. My theological studies came to a halt with an unexpected high-risk pregnancy and, as you know by now, a full-blown worldwide pandemic. However, the human condition is nothing new to any of us. We are flesh and blood, imperfect humans with not the best intentions all the time.

The difference for the Christian is that we know we cannot hide our intentions from God. We may plan and scheme against each other, knowing if we have hidden agendas or not, but God sees right through all of that. It is so important to constantly "check our hearts," but how do we do that? The first thing is to be honest with ourselves. To always examine the true intentions knowing that God is well aware of them no matter how well we "think" we can hide them. Being honest with God and ourselves is no easy task, and I speak from experience!

Here's the thing, if we do manage to fool people, we have to understand that even though there may not be any immediate consequences, it does not, by any means, mean that there will never be consequences; if not in this life, perhaps the next. Draw a heart—your version of a pure heart. It can be a literal heart or something that represents pureness in heart to you.

88

CHRIST + THE CREATIVE WORSHIPER

Create in me a pure heart, O God, and renew a steadfast spirit within me.
(Psalm 51:10 NIV)

Being a Christian artist comes with its fair share of criticism. Some are not so inclined and others, mostly artists, get the connection between creativity and God, but what I have learned over the years is that we cannot please everybody, and when we try to, we start to lose a little bit of ourselves.

We should always strive to continue to be transformed into a more Christ-like character. To allow Him to create a pure heart in us and to renew our spirit, but Christ also uses our personalities and interests for His glory. Sometimes there are things that we need to let go of, but God will guide you on what those are, and it's usually things that are harmful and things that draw you farther from God instead of closer to Him. With that said, let us take a look at Jesus Himself.

He was a carpenter, which required creativity. It is no wonder why creating the heavens, the earth, and every creature of the universe coincides with God-like characteristics that are seen in humans.

My husband works in the analyst/developer world, and he gets to create things with computer codes and languages. It fascinates me so much to see him work with such attention and focus. He is the more tech-savvy one in our marriage, and he has taken up the task of making a smart home out of this place. It is amazing to me that I can walk into my house and with my voice tell the lights to turn on, tell the tv to turn on, and the speakers to play music! So, I think, how could the God of the universe not speak life into existence if we only obtain a fraction of His image. God, in His fullest omnipresence and omnipotent nature, is well capable of creating and managing life and all the worlds with it.

So where am I going with all this? I am asking myself the same question. I guess my point is that being creative, if used to glorify God, should be celebrated as a gift from our creator. The rest of this sketchbook is left blank just for you. I want to thank you wholeheartedly, dear reader, for allowing me to share my devotions, my process, and a little bit of my soul with you. I truly, truly pray that this book has blessed you. That it has stirred up a newness within your spirit, that it has maybe added a little edification to your life. You have seen and experienced my way of "sketchbooking" and by all means keep going and following the same pattern of "Scripture," "Devotional," "Prayer," and last but certainly not least— "Artwork". You may very well discover your own template. Whatever it is that you decide to do with the rest of this sketchbook, may it be sweet to your spirit and refreshing to your mind. May it become an arrow in your quiver to stand against the wiles of the very present enemy in this spiritual war.

In His Love and Service,

—Laura

94

100

102

104

108

110

112

116

118

122

124

128

130

132

134

136

138

140

142

144

146

148

150

152

154

158

160

170

172

174

176

178

184

188

190

194

196

200

REFERENCES

Petterson, Eugene H. 2005. *The Message [MSG]*. Tyndale House Publishers, Inc. https://www.biblegateway.com/versions/Message-MSG-Bible/#booklist.

The Holy Bible: Living Bible [TLB]. 1971. Carol Stream, Illinois: Tyndale House Foundation. https://www.biblegateway.com/versions/The-Living-Bible-TLB/.

The Holy Bible: New International Version [NIV]. 1984. Grand Rapids: Zonderman Publishing House.https://www.biblegateway.com/versions/New-International-Version-NIV-Bible/#booklist.

The Holy Bible: The New King James Version [NKJV]. 1999. Nashville, TN: Thomas Nelson, Inc. https://www.biblegateway.com/versions/New-King-James-Version-NKJV-Bible/#booklist.

IN LOVING MEMORY

Fanny Lisbet Morales Garcia aka "Fan Fan"
You are dearly loved and missed, my sister in Christ,
but it's not goodbye... it's see you later!